PAR FOR THE COURSE

PAR FOR THE

Compiled by ERIC ZWEIG

COURSE

GOLF'S BEST
QUOTES AND QUIPS

FIREFLY BOOKS

A Firefly Book

Published by Firefly Books Ltd. 2007

First printing

PUBLISHER CATALOGING-IN-PUBLICATION DATA (U.S.)
Par for the course : golf's best quotes & quips / compiled by Eric Zweig
[176] p. : photos. (some col.) ;   cm.
Includes index.
Summary: Sarcastic, wise, witty and humorous quotes about golf.
ISBN-13: 978-1-55407-257-6 (pbk.)
ISBN-10: 1-55407-257-3 (pbk.)
1. Golf–Quotations, maxims, etc. 2. Golf–Humor. I. Zweig, Eric. II. Title.
796.352 dc22   GV967.P37 2007

LIBRARY AND ARCHIVES CANADA CATALOGUING IN PUBLICATION
Par for the course : golf's best quotes & quips / compiled by Eric Zweig.
Includes index.
ISBN-13: 978-1-55407-257-6
ISBN-10: 1-55407-257-3
1. Golf–Quotations, maxims, etc. 2. Golf–Humor. I. Zweig, Eric, 1963-
GV967.P37 2007   796.352   C2006-905597-1-7

Published in the United States by
Firefly Books (U.S.) Inc.
P.O. Box 1338, Ellicott Station
Buffalo, New York 14205

Published in Canada by
Firefly Books Ltd.
66 Leek Crescent
Richmond Hill, Ontario L4B 1H1

Cover and interior design by Sari Naworynski

Printed in Canada

The publisher gratefully acknowledges the financial support for our publishing program by the Government of Canada through the Book Publishing Industry Development Program.

For Zara and Jorey from their Uncle Bear.

CONTENTS

INTRODUCTION

> *"Turning to sports, winner of this week's Gulf Coast Golf Classic was Chi Chi Rodriquez. Chi Chi finished with a nine-under-par score. Hopefully, Mr. Rodriguez will play up to par in the next competition."*
>
> Newscaster Les Nessman (actor Richard Sanders)
> on *WKRP in Cincinnati*

I always thought that was pretty funny. (Of course, a lot of that has to do with the way Les mangles the name – Chy Chy Rodri-qweez. And, a lot of it also has to do with the fact that I watched way too much television growing up!) But as I was compiling the quotations for this book, I began to think it was pretty appropriate. Now, admittedly, I'm not a golfer (though I have watched plenty of it on television – see above) but I've started to wonder if maybe there's something about a pursuit in which you don't want to perform up to par that explains the love-hate relationship so many people seem to have with this game.

As in the book of baseball quotes I did for this series, I was not surprised to find that golf quotes cover a very broad range of subjects. After all, it has been said that the smaller the ball, the better the writing. So why shouldn't the same apply to the spoken word? Yet, like my football book, I found that the vast majority of golf quotes really only cover two topics: love and hate. (Another dominant topic is why the game is so hard, but really that's just a sub-heading for the other two.)

People can get quite poetic when describing what they love about golf. For example, movie legend Robert Redford sums up the feelings of many a golf lover when he says that golf is a wonderful metaphor for life "because you're playing against yourself and nature." Golf legend Arnold Palmer is no less eloquent when he maintains, "What other people may find in poetry or art museums, I find in the flight of a good drive." Golfer Bernhard Langer has a simpler explanation. "You know why the game of golf is so popular? Very easy. It's a great game."

Yet not everyone agrees.

Greg Norman's daughter Morgan-Leigh was once asked if she planned to follow her father out onto the links. "No way," she said. "Golf is too boring." And it seems that even golf lovers can hate the game. "I am a golfer," wrote American novelist Rex Beach in the foreword to the 1932 book *A New Way to Better Golf*. "I have played the game for twenty years, but I have recently made a discovery. I hate it!"

Of course, so much of what a golfer feels about the game depends on how he played that day. "After all," said legendary golf writer Herbert Warren Wind, "as every golfer in every land will attest after a good round, it may well be the best game ever invented." Then again, "by the time you get dressed, drive out there, play eighteen holes and come home, you've blown seven hours. There are better things you can do with your time." Richard Nixon said that.

So even if you hate golf, but especially if you love it, I hope you'll enjoy this book.

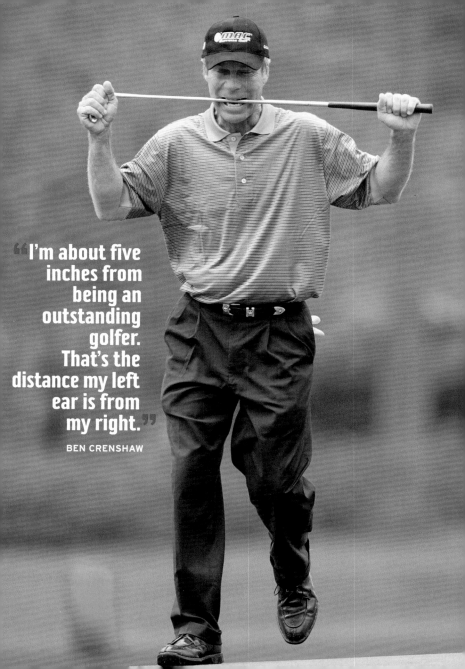

"I'm about five inches from being an outstanding golfer. That's the distance my left ear is from my right."

BEN CRENSHAW

"He was always on my case about thinking my way around the golf course and not letting emotions get the better of you. You just use your mind to plot your way around the golf course and if you have to deviate from the game plan, make sure it is the right decision to do that. He was very adamant I play like that my entire career."

TIGER WOODS, ON HIS LATE FATHER EARL

"It is impossible to outplay an opponent you can't outthink."

LAWSON LITTLE

"I always said you have to be really smart or really dumb to play this game well. I just don't know where I fit in."

BETH DANIEL

"Golf is a game that is played on a five-inch course – the distance between your ears."

GOLF LEGEND **BOBBY JONES**

"The worst club in my bag is my brain."

CHRIS PERRY

"After you've got the basics down, it's all mental."

KEN VENTURI

"Let's face it, **95 percent** of this game **is mental. A guy plays lousy golf** he doesn't need a pro, he needs a shrink."

SPORTSWRITER **TOM MURPHY**

"Everyone in golf has trouble with the mental side of the game, whether you're a pro or a 20-handicap. You get thoughts in your head all the time."

THREE-TIME CANADIAN AMATEUR CHAMPION
RICHARD SCOTT

"Frankly, I don't know what to think about it. Just thinking about it might upset my rhythm."

JYOTI RANDHAWA, LEADING A FIELD THAT INCLUDED 10 OF THE WORLD'S TOP 20 PLAYERS AFTER THE FIRST ROUND OF THE 2006 HSBC CHAMPIONS TOURNAMENT (HE FINISHED TIED FOR NINTH)

"A routine is not a routine if you have to think about it."

DAVIS LOVE JR.

"Someone once asked him what was tougher, football or golf. He said golf because in football you just react. In golf, there's too much time to think."

BOBBY GENOVESE, ON HIS FATHER BOBBY CUNNINGHAM JR. WHO PLAYED IN THE CANADIAN FOOTBALL LEAGUE IN THE 1940s AND 50s AND GOLFED PROFESSIONALLY IN CANADA AND THE UNITED STATES

"The simpler I keep things, the better I play."

NANCY LOPEZ

"Relax?

**How can anybody relax and play golf?
You have to grip
the club,
don't you?** "

GOLF GREAT
BEN HOGAN

"Golf combines two favorite American pastimes: taking long walks and hitting things with a stick."

POLITICAL SATIRIST **P.J. O'ROURKE**

"Golf is good for the soul. You get so mad at yourself you forget to hate your enemies."

HUMORIST **WILL ROGERS**

"They throw their clubs backwards, and that's wrong. You should always throw a club ahead of you so that you don't have to walk any extra distance to get it."

TOMMY BOLT ON THE TEMPERS OF OTHER PLAYERS

"Why do we work so hard to feel so terrible?"

HOLLIS STACY

"You must never forget that golf is supposed to be a game of relaxation. It should take your mind off your work, your mortgage, your income tax and introduce fresh and much more serious problems into your life."

STEPHEN BAKER

"Golf always makes me so damn angry."

KING GEORGE V OF ENGLAND

"The most charismatic figure I have ever seen, swinging, punching, slashing his way around the golf courses of the world."

BRITISH GOLF GREAT **PETER ALLISS** ON ARNOLD PALMER

"Arnold Palmer invented it about eight years ago in a little town outside Pittsburgh."

GOLF ADMINISTRATOR AND RULES EXPERT **FRANK HANNIGAN,** IN RESPONSE TO THE QUESTION "WHEN DID GOLF BEGIN?"

"When Arnold came along, there really weren't any stars in the game, and the game was greatly needing somebody to take charge, and he did."

JACK NICKLAUS ON ARNOLD PALMER

"His caveman approach took the audience by storm.

He was Cagney pushing a grapefruit in Mae Clark's face,

Gable kicking down the door to Scarlett O'Hara's bedroom."

LEGENDARY SPORTSWRITER JIM MURRAY ON ARNOLD PALMER

"I've always made a total effort, even when the odds seemed entirely against me. I never quit trying. I never felt that I didn't have a chance to win."

ARNOLD PALMER

"I have the utmost respect for Arnold Palmer. He is a wonderful player and person and he will always be my friend."

SEVE BALLESTEROS

"If I ever needed an eight foot putt, and everything I owned depended on it, I would want Arnold Palmer to putt for me."

GOLF LEGEND **BOBBY JONES**

"It's like riding a lion down the road, whipping him with a rattlesnake, while trying to get away from a mean guy behind you."

DOUG SANDERS ON PLAYING AGAINST ARNOLD PALMER

"He was in touch with the people who were watching him play. He looked everybody in the eye and everyone thought he was looking individually at them."

TOM WATSON ON ARNOLD PALMER

"He's a great model for all of us. He made golf what it is today. We look up to him not only for what he did for golf but for how he is as a person."

BERNARD LANGER ON ARNOLD PALMER

"I can sum it up like this: Thank God for the game of golf."

ARNOLD PALMER

"I've never been to heaven, and thinking back on my life, I probably won't get a chance to go. I guess the Masters is as close as I'm going to get."

FUZZY ZOELLER, AFTER WINNING THE 1979 MASTERS

"If you don't get goose bumps when you walk into this place, you don't have a pulse."

HAL SUTTON ON AUGUSTA NATIONAL, HOME OF THE MASTERS

"Watching the Masters on CBS is like attending a church service. Announcers speak in hushed, pious tones, as if to convince us that something of great meaning and historical importance is taking place. What we are actually seeing is grown men hitting little balls with sticks."

TOM GILMORE

"You don't come to Augusta to find your game. You come here because you've got one."

GOLF LEGEND **GENE SARAZEN** ON THE MASTERS

"The first time I played the Masters, I was so nervous I drank a bottle of rum before I teed off. I shot the happiest 83 of my life."

CHI CHI RODRIGUEZ

"Golf is so popular simply because it is the best game in the world at which to be bad."

BRITISH AUTHOR **A.A. MILNE**, BEST KNOWN FOR HIS BOOKS ABOUT WINNIE THE POOH

"I like golf because you can be really terrible at it and still not look much dorkier than anybody else."

HUMOR COLUMNIST **DAVE BARRY**

"My golf is woeful but I will never surrender."

ENTERTAINER AND GOLF ENTHUSIAST **BING CROSBY**

"My clubs are well used, but unfortunately not used well."

JACK BURRELL

"It is the constant and undying hope for improvement that makes golf so exquisitely worth playing."

LEGENDARY GOLF WRITER **BERNARD DARWIN**

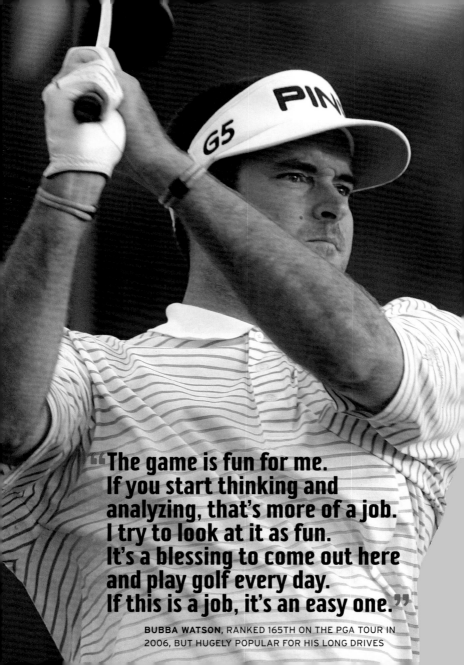

"The game is fun for me. If you start thinking and analyzing, that's more of a job. I try to look at it as fun. It's a blessing to come out here and play golf every day. If this is a job, it's an easy one."

BUBBA WATSON, RANKED 165TH ON THE PGA TOUR IN 2006, BUT HUGELY POPULAR FOR HIS LONG DRIVES

"I don't think of myself as a celebrity or superstar. I'm just an ordinary guy who makes his living in a crazy way. My only fear is that I may have to go out and get a real job."

FUZZY ZOELLER

"I'm vice president in charge of special marketing. That means I play golf and go to cocktail parties. I'm pretty good at my job."

BASEBALL LEGEND **MICKEY MANTLE**

"I love to play. I love fishing and hunting and trap-shooting and ping-pong and chess and pool and billiards and driving a motor-car, and at times I love golf, when I can get the shots going somewhere near the right. It seems I love almost any pursuit ... except work."

BOBBY JONES

"My wife said to me the other day, 'My God, you may get to 65 without ever working a day in your life.'"

JOHN BRODIE, AFTER JOINING THE SENIOR TOUR

"I don't know why that putt hung on the edge. I'm a clean liver. It must be my caddy."

JOANNE CARNER

"Caddies are a breed of their own. If you shoot 66, they say, 'Man, we shot 66!' But go out and shoot 77 and they say, 'Hell, he shot 77!'"

LEE TREVINO

"When I ask you what club to hit, look the other way and don't you dare say a word."

ADVICE FROM GOLF LEGEND **SAM SNEAD** TO HIS CADDY

"If I needed advice from my caddy, he'd be hitting the shots and I'd be carrying the bag."

BOBBY JONES

"When I make a bad shot, your job is to take the blame."

ADVICE FROM **SEVE BALLESTEROS** TO HIS CADDIES

"Golf is an awkward set of bodily contortions designed to produce a graceful result."

TOMMY ARMOUR

"The ideal build for a golfer would be strong hands, big forearms, thin neck, big thighs and a flat chest. He'd look like Popeye."

GARY PLAYER

"Give me a man with big hands and big feet and no brains and I'll make a golfer out of him."

GOLF LEGEND **WALTER HAGEN**

"If God wants to produce the ideal golfer then He should create a being with a set of unequal arms and likewise legs, an elbow-free left arm, knees which hinge sideways and a ribless torso from which emerges, at an angle of 45 degrees, a stretched neck fitted with one color-blind eye stuck firmly on the left side."

GOLF WRITER **CHRIS PLUMRIDGE**

"From the beginning it was drilled into me that a golf course was a place where character fully reveals itself – both its strengths and its flaws. As a result, I learned early not only to fix my ball marks but also to congratulate an opponent on a good shot, avoid walking ahead of a player preparing to shoot, remain perfectly still when someone else was playing, and a score of other small courtesies that revealed, in my father's mind, one's abiding respect for the game."

ARNOLD PALMER

"Golf asks something of a man. It makes one loathe mediocrity. It seems to say, 'If you are going to keep company with me, don't embarrass me.'"

SOUTH AFRICAN STAR **GARY PLAYER**

"The man who can go into a patch of rough alone, with the knowledge that only God is watching him, and play his ball where it lies, is the man who will serve you faithfully and well."

ENGLISH COMIC WRITER **P.G. WODEHOUSE**

"Eighteen holes of match or medal play will teach you more about your foe than will 18 years of dealing with him across a desk."

LEGENDARY SPORTSWRITER GRANTLAND RICE

"Golf puts a man's character on the anvil and his richest qualities – patience, poise and restraint – to the flame."

BILLY CASPER

"I don't know very much. I know a little about golf. I know how to make a stew. And I know how to be a decent man."

GOLF LEGEND BYRON NELSON

"Always remember that you have an obligation to protect the integrity and traditions of the game. It's important... The responsibility is all on your shoulders. Protect the game. It's beautiful."

ARNOLD PALMER TO TIGER WOODS AT THE 1997 PGA TOUR'S AWARDS DINNER

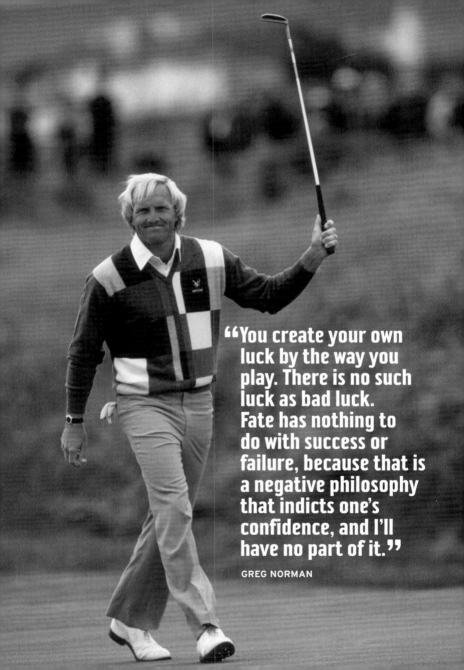

"You create your own luck by the way you play. There is no such luck as bad luck. Fate has nothing to do with success or failure, because that is a negative philosophy that indicts one's confidence, and I'll have no part of it."

GREG NORMAN

"Confidence is everything. From there, it's a small step to winning."

CRAIG STADLER

"It takes hundreds of good golf shots to gain confidence, but only one bad one to lose it."

JACK NICKLAUS

"I just stepped up, told myself I'd made a thousand of them or more in my career, and rolled it in."

JOHN ROLLINS ON HIS FIVE-FOOT BIRDIE PUTT TO WIN THE 2006 B.C. OPEN

"I've done it before, and that's the thing. If you've won doing it that way, it always gives you confidence to know that you can do that again."

TIGER WOODS, WHO HAS NEVER LOST A MAJOR CHAMPIONSHIP WHEN LEADING AFTER 54 HOLES, ON THE FACT THAT 14 PLAYERS WERE WITHIN FIVE SHOTS OF HIM HEADING INTO THE FINAL DAY OF THE 2006 BRITISH OPEN

"Talking to a golf ball won't do you any good, unless you do it while your opponent is teeing off."

AUTHOR **BRUCE LANSKY**

"The loudest sound you hear is the guy jangling coins to distract a player he bet against."

LEGENDARY SPORTSWRITER **JIM MURRAY** ON GOLF

"Someone who jingles coins in his pockets. On a cold day especially. It's worse then because they all have their hands in their pockets. It sounds like the checkout counter at the Piggly Wiggly."

J.C. SNEAD ON WHAT BOTHERS HIM MOST ON THE GOLF COURSE

"It's so ridiculous to see a golfer with a one-foot putt and everybody is saying "Shhh" and not moving a muscle. Then we allow nineteen-year-old kids to face a game-deciding free throw with seventeen thousand people yelling."

COLLEGE BASKETBALL COACH-TURNED-COMMENTATOR **AL McGUIRE**

"I don't like to watch golf on television. I can't stand whispering."

COMEDIAN **DAVID BRENNER**

**"You can't call it a sport.
You don't run,
jump,
you don't shoot,
you don't pass.
All you have to do
is buy some clothes
that don't match."**

BASEBALL PLAYER **STEVE SAX**

"Knickers are good for my golf game. They're cooler in hot weather, because the air circulates in them and they're warmer in cold weather because they trap the body heat."

PAYNE STEWART

"To play golf you need goofy pants and a fat ass."

ACTOR **ADAM SANDLER** AS HAPPY GILMORE

"I'd give up golf if I didn't have so many sweaters."

COMEDIAN **BOB HOPE** AFTER HITTING AN ERRANT TEE SHOT AT A PRO-AM

"'Play it as it lies' is one of the fundamental dictates of golf. The other is 'Wear it if it clashes.'"

HUMORIST **HENRY BEARD**

"Although golf was originally restricted to wealthy, overweight Protestants, today it's open to anybody who owns hideous clothing."

HUMOR WRITER **DAVE BARRY**

"That whacko Swede in his silly cap and skinny tap dancer's pants always looks like the last guy to climb out of the clown car at the circus."

WRITER **DAN JENKINS** ON JESPER PARNEVIK

"I feel calm in calm colors. I don't want people to watch the way I dress. I want people to watch the way I play."

SEVE BALLESTEROS

"The last thing you want to do is shoot 80 wearing 'tartan troosers.'"

BRITISH GOLFER **IAN POULTER**

"When you get up there in years, the fairways get longer and the holes get smaller."

SOUTH AFRICAN GOLF STAR **BOBBY LOCKE**

"The older you get the stronger the wind gets... and it's always in your face."

JACK NICKLAUS

"The older you get, the easier it is to shoot your age."

JERRY BARBER

"That's the easiest 69 I ever made."

WALTER HAGEN, ON TURNING 69

The older I get, the better I used to be.

LEE TREVINO

"You know you're on the Senior Tour when your back goes out more than you do."

BOB BRUCE

"That's life. The older you get, the tougher it is to score."

COMEDIAN **BOB HOPE**

"What's nice about our tour is you can't remember your bad shots."

BOB BRUCE, ON THE SENIOR TOUR

"Palmer and Player played superbly, but Nicklaus played a game with which I am not familiar."

GOLF LEGEND BOBBY JONES ON JACK NICKLAUS

"The biggest thing is to have the mind-set and the belief that you can win every tournament going in. A lot of guys don't have that. Nicklaus had it... He felt he was going to beat everybody."

TIGER WOODS ON JACK NICKLAUS

"Around a clubhouse they'll tell you even God has to practice his putting. In fact, even Nicklaus does."

LEGENDARY SPORTSWRITER JIM MURRAY

"When he plays well, he wins. When he plays badly, he finishes second. When he plays terribly, he finishes third."

JOHNNY MILLER ON JACK NICKLAUS

"Nothing breaks his concentration. He can almost will the ball into the hole."

BEN CRENSHAW ON JACK NICKLAUS

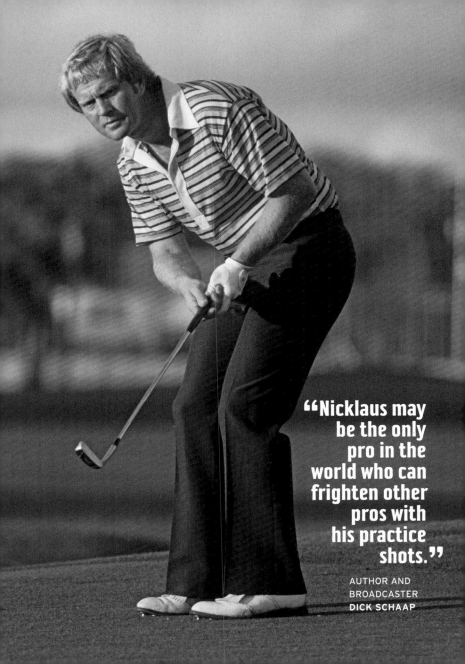

"Nicklaus may be the only pro in the world who can frighten other pros with his practice shots."

AUTHOR AND
BROADCASTER
DICK SCHAAP

"Golf is like eating. It's something which has to come naturally."

SAM SNEAD

"Golf is a game where guts, stick-to-it-iveness and blind devotion will get you nothing but an ulcer."

TOMMY BOLT

"Golf is like a love affair. If you don't take it seriously, it's no fun; if you do take it seriously, it breaks your heart."

ENGLISH WRITER **ARNOLD DALY**

"A game in which one endeavors to control a ball with implements ill adapted for the purposes."

U.S. PRESIDENT **WOODROW WILSON**

"A game in which a ball 1 1/2 inches in diameter is placed on a ball 8,000 miles in diameter. The object is to hit the small ball but not the larger."

WRITER **JOHN CUNNINGHAM**

"One hundred years of experience has demonstrated that the game is temporary insanity practiced in a pasture."

SPORTSWRITER **DAVE KINDRED**

"Playing golf is like chasing a quinine pill around a cow pasture."

SIR WINSTON CHURCHILL

"Golf is, in part, a game; but only in part. It is also in part a religion, a fever, a vice, a mirage, a frenzy, a fear, an abscess, a joy, a thrill, a pest, a disease, an uplift, a brooding, a melancholy, a dream of yesterday, and a hope for tomorrow."

NEW YORK TRIBUNE (1916)

"Golf is typical capitalist lunacy."

PLAYWRIGHT **GEORGE BERNARD SHAW**

"Golf is not a game of great shots. It's a game of the most misses. The people who win make the smallest mistakes."

GENE LITTLE

"Golf is like a chain. You always have to work on the weakest links."

GEORGE ARCHER

"Golf is 20 percent talent and 80 percent management."

BEN HOGAN

"Golf is just a game –and an idiotic game most of the time."

MARK CALCAVECCHIA

"Golf is an insurmountable game in which one attempts to put an insignificant ball into an obscure hole with an absurd weapon."

HARRY B. TROUT

"Don Quixote would understand golf. It is the impossible dream."

LEGENDARY SPORTSWRITER **JIM MURRAY**

"Golf is a lot of walking, broken up by disappointment and bad arithmetic.

JOURNALIST **EARL WILSON**

"Golf seems to me an arduous way to go for a walk. I prefer to take the dogs out."

PRINCESS ANNE OF ENGLAND

"Golf is a good walk spoiled."

AUTHOR **MARK TWAIN**

"Golf is not, and never has been, a fair game."

JACK NICKLAUS

"Golf is a puzzle without an answer."

GARY PLAYER

"Golf tips are like aspirins.
One may do you good,
but if you swallow the whole bottle
you will be lucky to survive."

GOLF COACH **HARVEY PENICK**

"I don't trust doctors. They are like golfers. Every one has a different answer to your problem."

SEVE BALLESTEROS

"You see the practice ground out there? It is an evil place. It's full of so-called coaches waiting to pounce on young guys or players who have lost their form. They just hope they can make money out of them. You can see them waiting to dish their mumbo-jumbo. I feel very sorry for those who are taken in because it can destroy everything that has brought them this far. To hell with coaches."

ERNIE ELS

"I have a tip that can take five strokes off anyone's golf game: it's called an eraser."

ARNOLD PALMER

"Golf is the most over-taught and

If they taught sex the way they teach golf,

least-learned human endeavor.

the race would have died out years ago."

LEGENDARY SPORTSWRITER **JIM MURRAY**

If you can hit the ball in the hole regularly by standing on your head, then keep right on – and don't listen to advice from anyone.

ENGLISH GOLF PRO **JOHN JACOBS**

"The difference between a sand trap and water is the difference between a car crash and an airplane crash. You have a chance of recovering from a car crash."

BOBBY JONES

"Golf balls are attracted to water as unerringly as the eye of a middle-aged man to a female bosom."

WRITER **MICHAEL GREEN**

"I'm hitting the woods just great ... but I'm having a terrible time getting out of them."

HARRY TOSCANO

"One under a tree, one under a bush, one under the water."

LEE TREVINO, DESCRIBING HOW HE WAS ONE UNDER DURING A TOURNAMENT

"The best advice I can give for playing a ball out of water is – don't."

TONY LEMA

"I'd like to see the fairways more narrow. Then everybody would have to play from the rough, not just me."

SEVE BALLESTEROS

"A rough should have high grass. When you go bowling they don't give you anything for landing in the gutter, do they?"

LEE TREVINO

"If I had my way, I'd never let the sand be raked. Instead, I'd run herd of elephants through the bunkers every morning."

GOLF COURSE DESIGNER **CHARLES BLAIR MacDONALD**

"Of all the hazards, fear is the worst."

GOLF LEGEND **SAM SNEAD**

"Golf is a stupid game. You tee up this little ball, really this tiny ball. Then you hit it, try to find it, hit it. And the goal is to get it into a little hole placed in a hard spot."

JULI INKSTER

"I accept the fact that I'm going to miss it sometimes. I just hope I miss it where I can find it."

FUZZY ZOELLER

"What goes up must come down. But don't expect it to come down where you can find it."

COMEDIAN **LILY TOMLIN**

"Hit it hard. It will land somewhere."

MARK CALCAVECCHIA

"Sometimes things don't go your way, and that's the way things go."

TIGER WOODS

"A golf ball is like a clock. Always hit it at 6 o'clock and make it go toward 12 o'clock. But make sure you're in the same time zone."

CHI CHI RODRIGUEZ

"If it wasn't for golf, I'd probably be a caddy today."

GEORGE ARCHER

"I owe a lot to my parents, especially my mother and my father."

GREG NORMAN

"If Olympic Club were human, it'd be Bela Lugosi. I think it turns into a bat at midnight."

LEGENDARY SPORTSWRITER JIM MURRAY

"Harbour Town is so tough, even your clubs get tired."

WRITER **CHARLES PRICE**

"The way I putted, I must have been reading the greens in Spanish and putting them in English."

HOMERO BLANCAS

"After all these years, it's still embarrassing for me to play on the American golf tour. Like the time I asked my caddy for a sand wedge and he came back ten minutes later with a ham on rye."

PUERTO RICAN STAR **CHI CHI RODRIQUEZ** ON HIS ACCENT

"That's as bad as getting back together with an ex-wife."

JOHN DALY, WHO'S NOW BEEN DIVORCED FOUR TIMES, AFTER A POOR SHOT AT THE 2006 TELUS SKINS GAME IN BANFF, ALBERTA

"If some players took a fork to their mouths the way they take the club back, they'd starve to death."

SAM SNEAD

"If you hit a ball with a mashie, it will sometimes go further than if you miss it with a driver."

LEGENDARY SPORTSWRITER **RING LARDNER**

"My career started off slowly and then tapered off."

GARY McCORD

"He must be amphibious."

BRITISH GOLFER **MARK JAMES** AFTER SERGIO GARCIA
THREW A BALL INTO THE GALLERY WITH HIS LEFT HAND

"We were on the ninth hole when he just teed off, and just listening to that ovation they gave him on the first, I was getting, what do you call it, chicken pops."

SPANISH WHIZ KID **SERGIO GARCIA** ON PLAYING AT THE
MASTERS DURING ARNOLD PALMER'S LAST ROUND THERE
IN 2002

"This hole is worse than trigonometry."

HUBIE GREEN, DESCRIBING NUMBER 9 AT PEBBLE BEACH

"**I play in the low 80s.
If it's
any hotter
than that,
I won't play.**"

COMEDIAN **JOE E. LEWIS**

"Wind, hole design and a hundred other factors in golf mean that you never hit the same shot two times in a row."

PHIL MICKELSON

"A man may be the best player and still he cannot win the championship unless the luck be with him."

LEGENDARY GOLF WRITER **BERNARD DARWIN**

"I don't care what anybody says. The first tournament is not the hardest to win. It's always the second one."

JOHN DALY

"It is nothing new or original to say that golf is played one stroke at a time. But it took me many years to realize it."

BOBBY JONES

"Golf is not a game of good shots. It's a game of bad shots."

GOLF LEGEND **BEN HOGAN**

"Golf gives you an insight into human nature, your own as well as your opponent's."

LEGENDARY SPORTSWRITER **GRANTLAND RICE**

"Forget your opponents. Always play against par."

SAM SNEAD

"I once thought of becoming a political cartoonist because they only have to come up with one idea a day. Then I thought I'd become a sportswriter instead, because they don't have to come up with any."

SAM SNEAD

"The best wood in most amateurs' bags is the pencil."

CHI CHI RODRIQUEZ

"Like unhitching a horse from a plow and winning the Derby."

LEGENDARY SPORTSWRITER **JIM MURRAY** ON ORVILLE MOODY'S UNEXPECTED WIN AT THE 1969 U.S. OPEN

"He's like a poodle out in front of all those Rottweilers."

CBS COMMENTATOR **GARY McCORD** AS JIM FURYK TRIED TO HOLD THE LEAD OVER SEVERAL LONG HITTERS AT THE 2006 WORLD GOLF CHAMPIONSHIP

"Twelve guys – three of them are firing a 50-millimeter cannon and nine guys are shooting BB guns."

TV ANALYST **JOHNNY MILLER** ON THE POOR PERFORMANCE BY THE U.S. TEAM AT THE 2006 RYDER CUP

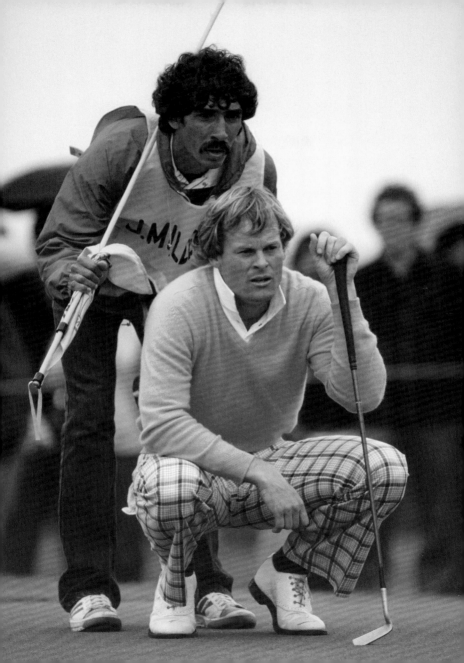

"He was so ugly as a kid that his parents tied pork chops around his neck so that the dog would play with him."

LEE TREVINO ON FELLOW GOLFER J.C. SNEAD

"Art said he wanted to get more distance. I told him to hit it and run backward."

KEN VENTURI, ON THE ADVICE HE GAVE TO LONGTIME SPORTSWRITER ART ROSENBAUM

"Bob Hope has a beautiful short game. Unfortunately, it's off the tee."

JIMMY DEMARET

"You've just one problem. You stand too close to the ball ... after you've hit it."

SAM SNEAD

"Ben Crenshaw hits in the woods so often, he should get an orange hunting jacket."

TOM WEISKOPF

"Al looks like the world's longest chimney sweep. He's around seven feet tall and could use his wedding ring for a belt. A 2-iron that talks."

LEGENDARY SPORTSWRITER **JIM MURRAY** ON AL GEIBERGER

"They call it **golf** because

all the other four letter words were taken. "

RAYMOND FLOYD

"I used to go to the driving range to practice driving without slicing. Now I go to the driving range to practice slicing without swearing."

AUTHOR **BRUCE LANSKY**

"If profanity had an influence on the flight of the ball, the game of golf would be played far better than it is."

ENGLISH GOLF WRITER **HORACE G. HUTCHINSON**

"I was afraid to move my lips in front of the TV cameras. The commissioner probably would have fined me just for what I was thinking."

TOM WEISKOPF, AFTER SHOOTING A 13 ON THE TWELFTH HOLE DURING THE 1980 MASTERS

"Golf is a game of expletives not deleted."

DR. IRVING A. GLADSTONE

"Fame is addictive. Money is addictive. Attention is addictive. But golf is second to none."

MUSICIAN **MARC ANTHONY**

"My divorce came as a complete surprise. That's what happens when you haven't been home in 18 years."

LEE TREVINO

"I'm a golfaholic, no question about that. Counseling wouldn't help me. They'd have to put me in prison, and then I'd talk the warden into building a hole or two and teach him how to play."

LEE TREVINO

"My conscience hurt me. I hate to play golf when I should be out working, so the only thing to do was quit working."

JIM UMBRACHT

"Someone once told me that there is more to life than golf. I think it was my ex-wife."

AUTHOR **BRUCE LANSKY**

"If I had to choose between my wife and my putter ... well, I'd miss her."

GARY PLAYER

Golf is the crack of sports.
Once I took it seriously, I loved it.
It absolutely saved my life.

ROCKER **ALICE COOPER**, WHO SAYS PLAYING GOLF HELPED HIM KICK HIS DRUG HABIT

"A lot of my buddies also played golf, but when it came to going to the beach or on the boat and chasing girls, they usually went that way and I went to the golf course."

MIKE WEIR

"I don't like going to the mall. I'm not really like the other girls. I just like to go out on the golf course and play. Golf is fun and feels really good."

MICHELLE WIE

"Golf is my boyfriend right now."

KARRIE WEBB

"The ardent golfer would play Mount Everest if somebody put a flagstick on top."

GOLF COURSE ARCHITECT **PETE DYE**

"I couldn't wait for the sun to come up the next morning so that I could get out on the course again."

BEN HOGAN

"Don't play too much golf. Two rounds a day are plenty."

HARRY VARDON

"I play golf with friends sometimes, but there are never friendly games."

BEN HOGAN

"When you are ahead, don't take it easy. Kill them. After the finish, then be a sportsman."

EARL WOODS TO HIS SON TIGER

"On the golf course you can't feel sorry for anyone. You have to try to win the golf tournament. You're not beating the guy you're playing against, you're playing against the course."

ERNIE ELS

"I never rooted against an opponent, but I never rooted for him either."

ARNOLD PALMER

"I look into their eyes, shake their hand, pat their back, and wish them luck, but I am thinking, 'I am going to bury you.'"

SEVE BALLESTEROS

"How would you like to
meet the top 143 people

at what you do each week
in order to survive?"

BRUCE CRAMPTON ON PLAYING ON THE PGA TOUR

"Golf is a game in which you yell 'Fore,' shoot six, and write down five."

BROADCASTER **PAUL HARVEY**

"A great handicap for some golfers is honesty."

CEO, BUSINESS COLUMNIST AND BESTSELLING AUTHOR
HARVEY MACKAY

"I've seen lifelong friends drift apart over golf just because one could play better, but the other counted better."

HUMORIST **STEPHEN LEACOCK**

"If there is any larceny in a man, golf will bring it out."

WRITER **PAUL GALLICO**

"The income tax has made more liars out of the American people than golf has."

HUMORIST **WILL ROGERS**

"Golf is a game in which the ball lies poorly and the players well."

SPORTSWRITER **ART ROSENBAUM**

"Most people play a fair game of golf – if you watch them."

COMEDIAN **JOEY ADAMS**

"Golf is like solitaire. When you cheat, you only cheat yourself."

TONY LEMA

"Golf is the hardest game in the world to play, and the easiest to cheat at."

DAVE HILL

"When you see her hit a golf ball ...
there's nothing that prepares you for it.
It's just the scariest thing you've ever seen."

FRED COUPLES ON MICHELLE WIE,
WHO WAS DRIVING THE BALL 280 YARDS AT THE AGE OF 16

"There are no short hitters on the tour anymore –
just long and unbelievably long."

SAM SNEAD, ON HOW GOLF HAD CHANGED SINCE HIS DAY

"You guys place more emphasis on length than we
do. I don't look at a scorecard and say, 'Oh my God,
it's 7,561 yards.' I look at the first hole and it's 434
yards, and what do I have to do to hit on the green?"

JEFF SLUMAN ON THE MEDIA'S FASCINATION WITH THE
RECORD LENGTH OF THE MEDINAH COUNTRY CLUB COURSE,
USED FOR THE 2006 PGA CHAMPIONSHIP

"It's kind of like moving to a new neighborhood
where everybody wants to build a bigger house
than the last guy who built one."

JIM FURYK, ON THE FACT THAT GOLF COURSES ARE
GETTING LONGER AND LONGER

"His driving is unbelievable. I don't go that far on my holidays."

IAN BAKER-FINCH, ON JOHN DALY

"I can airmail the golf ball, but sometimes I don't put the right address on it."

JIM DENT, WHO WAS THE LONGEST HITTER ON THE PGA TOUR BUT NOT THE MOST ACCURATE

"Grip it and rip it. It works for John Daly. It never worked for me. All I did was wear out golf gloves."

WRITER/EDITOR **CHUCK STARK**

"John certainly gives it a good hit, doesn't he? My Sunday best is a Wednesday afternoon compared to him."

NICK FALDO, ON JOHN DALY

"I enjoy the oohs! and aahs! from the gallery when I hit my drives. But I'm getting pretty tired of the awws! and uhhs! when I miss the putt."

JOHN DALY

"Drive for show, but putt for dough."

BOBBY LOCKE

"I don't think people appreciate how hard we work, and mentally how hard it is to win a Major."

NICK FALDO

"I'm going to go down in history books not so much for the 165 tournaments I've won, including the Masters three times, the PGA National three times and the British Open once, but for the one tournament I never won. I'll tell you a little secret though, I think the fact I never won the U.S. Open kind of endears me to golf fans. Some, anyway. They'd come out and root for me, bless them, and my impossible dream in a way became theirs too."

SAM SNEAD

"I can't believe I did that. I am such an idiot. I just couldn't hit a fairway all day."

PHIL MICKELSON, AFTER A DOUBLE-BOGEY ON THE FINAL HOLE HANDED THE 2006 U.S. OPEN TO GEOFF OGILVY

"I'm 42 years old. I've been doing this for 19 years. It's the PGA Championship. Why not me?"

BILLY ANDRADE, WHO WAS AMONG FOUR GOLFERS TIED FOR THE LEAD THROUGH 36 HOLES AT THE 2006 PGA CHAMPIONSHIP (HE ENDED UP 18 SHOTS BEHIND TIGER WOODS)

"At my age, I've got to look positively. I'm 43 next week and it's nice that I can come back after nine years since contending for this tournament and do well again. I look forward to coming back again next year and try for another U.S. Open ... disaster."

EUROPEAN TOUR VETERAN **COLIN MONTGOMERIE**, AFTER BOTCHING THE FINAL HOLE AND COSTING HIMSELF AT LEAST A CHANCE AT A PLAYOFF AT THE 2006 U.S. OPEN

"You hear these guys saying, 'Oh, I can't play this course; it doesn't suit my game,' but that's the biggest bunch of rubbish I ever heard. The whole idea of golf is that you have to adapt your game to the course you're playing."

JACK NICKLAUS ON GOLFERS WHO DON'T LIKE PLAYING THE ENGLISH LINKS COURSES AT THE BRITISH OPEN

"Hell, it ain't like losing a leg."

BILLY JOE PATTON AFTER LOSING THE MASTERS

"I'm disappointed, but I'm not going to run around like Dennis Rodman and head-butt somebody."

GREG NORMAN ON LOSING A SIX-STROKE LEAD AT THE MASTERS

"The mystery of golf is that nobody can master it. You can shoot a good score today, but can you do it tomorrow?"

CURTIS STRANGE

"Golf is assuredly a mystifying game. It would seem that if a person has hit a golf ball correctly a thousand times, he should be able to duplicate the performance at will. But this is certainly not the case."

BOBBY JONES

"My favorite shots are the practice swing and the conceded putt. The rest can never be mastered."

ONETIME BRITISH DEFENSE SECRETARY AND NATO SECRETARY-GENERAL **LORD ROBERTSON**

"Golf is the hardest game in the world. There is no way you can ever get it. Just when you think you do, the game jumps up and puts you in your place."

BEN CRENSHAW

"No one has ever conquered this game. One week out there and you are God, next time you are the devil. But it does keep you coming back."

JULI INKSTER

"I have always had a drive that pushes me to try for perfection, and golf is a game in which perfection stays just out of reach."

LPGA GREAT **BETSY RAWLS**

"Always remember that however good you may be, the game is your master."

J.H. TAYLOR

"The more you play it the less you know about it."

LPGA LEGEND **PATTY BERG**

"One thing about golf is you don't know why you play bad and why you play good."

GEORGE ARCHER

"One minute
        you're bleeding.
The next minute
        you're hemorrhaging.
The next minute you're
        painting the
Mona Lisa."

MAC O'GRADY, DESCRIBING A TYPICAL ROUND OF GOLF

**"It's the most humbling sport ever.
It's like a lousy lover.
It's like some guy who's never
there when you need him.
Every once in a while,
he comes and makes you feel
like heaven on earth.
And then the moment you say,
'I really need this,' he's gone."**

ENTERTAINER AND GOLF ENTHUSIAST **DINAH SHORE**

"Golf is a game you can never get too good at. You can improve, but you can never get to where you master the game."

GAY BREWER

"Golf is a game in which attitude of mind counts for incomparably more than mightiness of muscle."

WRITER ARNOLD HAULTAIN

"Golf is a spiritual game. It's like Zen. You have to let your mind take over."

AMY ALCOTT

"A lot of people think I am cold and have no feelings. But I do. I just try very hard to focus and not let my emotions take over on the golf course."

ANNIKA SORENSTAM

"You have to train the mind for success. When I first joined the Tour, I didn't think I was as good as I was. Now my mental game has caught up with my physical game."

CALVIN PEETE

"If I ever think anybody is better than me, then I can never be the best. I always have to believe I'm the best."

TWO-TIME U.S. OPEN CHAMP PAYNE STEWART

"Staying in the present is the key to any golfer's game. Once you start thinking about a shot you just messed up or what you have to do on the next nine to catch somebody, you're lost."

PAUL AZINGER

"The more good rounds you play on a golf course, the more good memories you have to draw upon when you need to."

MIKE WEIR

"You need a fantastic memory in this game to remember the great shots and a very short memory to forget the bad ones."

MAC O'GRADY

"The mind messes up more shots than the body."

TOMMY BOLT

"For this game you need, above all things, to be in a tranquil frame of mind."

GOLF LEGEND HARRY VARDON

"The only stats I care about are paychecks and victories."

GREG NORMAN

"Victory is everything. You can spend the money, but you can never spend the memories."

KEN VENTURI

"Why? I can think of a million reasons."

TIGER WOODS, WHEN QUESTIONED AS TO WHY HE WOULD RATHER WIN THE AMERICAN EXPRESS CHAMPIONSHIP (WITH ITS $1 MILLION FIRST PRIZE) THAN THE 2002 RYDER CUP

"I'm going to win so much money this year, my caddy will make the top twenty money-winners' list."

LEE TREVINO, HEADING INTO THE 1973 SEASON

"My dad gave me great advice and I have never really played for money. I never thought that, 'Well, this is a $100,000 putt' or 'This tournament is worth $1 million' or 'I need to move into the top 10 so I can make more money.' But this year I've been playing for points and it's really been a distraction."

DAVIS LOVE III, ON TRYING TO QUALIFY FOR THE 2006 U.S. RYDER CUP TEAM

"Walter Hagen was the first player I knew that earned $1 million from golf, and of course he spent it, too. Sam Snead earned $1 million, too – and he saved $2 million."

GOLF PROMOTER **FRED CORCORAN**

"I never wanted to be a millionaire. I just wanted to live like one."

WALTER HAGEN

"The only reason I ever played golf in the first place was so I could afford to hunt and fish."

SAM SNEAD

"When I was playing regularly, I had a goal. I could see the prize money going into the ranch, buying a tractor, or a cow. It gave me incentive."

BYRON NELSON

"When I first came on tour, I was playing for money. Now I'm playing to win golf tournaments and the money is more than I ever dreamed I could make."

ANNIKA SORENSTAM

"I did not ever dream in my wildest imagination there would be as much money or that people would hit the ball so far. I only won $182,000 in my whole life. In 1937, I got fifth-place money at the British Open – $187 – and it cost me $3,000 to play because I had to take a one-month leave of absence from my club job to go."

BYRON NELSON

"To be truthful, I think golfers are overpaid. It's unreal, and I have trouble dealing with the guilt sometime."

COLIN MONTGOMERIE

"The world's number one tennis player spends 90 percent of his time winning, while the world's number one golfer spends 90 percent of his time losing. Golfers are great losers."

IRISH GOLFER **DAVID FEHERTY**

"I'm playing pretty good now, but my ranking doesn't say that. I'm number two."

VIJAY SINGH

"It's a heck of a lot harder to stay on top than it is to get there."

TOM KITE

"I'm wondering if anyone is going to put an asterisk on it because Tiger didn't play enough rounds."

JIM FURYK, WHO FINISHED THE 2006 PGA TOUR RANKED SECOND TO TIGER WOODS, BUT BEAT HIM OUT FOR THE VARDON TROPHY FOR THE LOWEST ADJUSTED SCORING AVERAGE BECAUSE WOODS DID NOT PLAY IN THE MINIMUM OF 60 OFFICIAL ROUNDS NEEDED TO QUALIFY FOR THE AWARD

"Second doesn't matter. Second is about as important as fifty-second. Winning is the reason you're playing."

ARNOLD PALMER

"Nobody ever remembers who finished second at anything."

JACK NICKLAUS

"In golf, as in no other sport, your principal opponent is yourself."

LEGENDARY SPORTSWRITER **HERBERT WARREN WIND**

"Golf is the only-est sport. You're completely alone with every conceivable opportunity to defeat yourself. Golf brings out your assets and liabilities as a person. The longer you play, the more certain you are that a man's performance is the outward manifestation of who, in his heart, he really thinks he is."

HALE IRWIN

"In almost all other games, you pit yourself against a mortal foe. In golf, it is yourself against the world."

WRITER **ARNOLD HAULTAIN**

"The object of golf is to beat someone. Make sure that someone is not yourself."

BOBBY JONES

The only thing I miss about team sports is the camaraderie, the togetherness. Out here, it's just you and the ball.

MIKE WEIR, WHO PLAYED HOCKEY GROWING UP IN CANADA

"I screwed up. It's all on me. I know that. But losing this Masters is not the end of the world. I let this one get away, but I still have a pretty good life. I'll wake up tomorrow, still breathing, I hope. All these hiccups I have, they must be for a reason. All this is just a test. I just don't know what the test is yet."

GREG NORMAN ON THE TOUGHEST OF HIS MANY TOUGH LOSSES AT THE 1996 MASTERS

"Golf is a choke game. Nobody every shanked a three-iron because his opponent threw him a curve or put too much topspin on the ball. When Scott Hoch missed a three-foot putt to blow the 1989 Masters, the ball was sitting perfectly still when he hit it and the crowd was perfectly silent. It was completely, entirely, totally him. That's why golf is also the cruelest game."

SPORTSWRITER MARK MULVOY

"If you're caught on a golf course during a storm and are afraid of lightning, hold up a one-iron. Not even God can hit a one-iron."

LEE TREVINO

"Actually, the only time I ever took out a one-iron was to kill a tarantula. And I took a seven to do that."

LEGENDARY SPORTSWRITER **JIM MURRAY**

"Never bet with anyone you meet on the first tee who has a deep suntan, a one-iron in his bag, and squinty eyes."

DAVE MARR

"The one-iron is almost unplayable. You keep it in your bag the way you keep a Dostoyevsky novel in your bookcase – with the vague notion that you will try it someday. In the meantime, it impresses your friends."

GOLF WRITERS **TOM SCOTT** AND **GEOFFREY COUSINS**

"A good one-iron shot is about as easy to come by as an understanding wife."

WRITER **DAN JENKINS**

"Golf is the easiest sport to look foolish at. I mean if I bat against Roger Clemens, I'll look foolish. But if I bat against someone of equal ability, I might not look so bad. In golf, though, it looks so simple, and then you have to hit this stationary ball."

HOCKEY LEGEND **WAYNE GRETZKY**

"It's a lot easier hitting a quarterback than a little white ball."

HALL OF FAME DEFENSIVE LINEMAN **BUBBA SMITH**

"I was three over. One over a house, one over a patio, and one over a swimming pool."

BASEBALL HALL OF FAMER **GEORGE BRETT**

"It took me seventeen years to get 3,000 hits in baseball. I did it in one afternoon on the golf course."

BASEBALL HALL OF FAMER **HANK AARON**

"But you don't have to go up in the stands and play your foul balls. I do."

SAM SNEAD, TO BASEBALL GREAT TED WILLIAMS DURING AN ARGUMENT AS TO WHETHER IT WAS MORE DIFFICULT TO HIT A MOVING BASEBALL OR A STATIONARY GOLF BALL

"Swing hard in case you hit it."

HALL OF FAME QUARTERBACK **DAN MARINO**

"I think golf is good for boxing, but the reverse is far from the case."

MAX BAER, HEAVYWEIGHT CHAMPION IN THE MID 1930s

"When you're just not very good at something, it's sometimes hard to justify spending six hours to do it."

SIX-TIME TOUR DE FRANCE CYCLING CHAMPION
LANCE ARMSTRONG ON GOLF

"I went to go get hypnotized so I would get rid of the yips in my golf swing. All I got was a good nap."

NBA GREAT **CHARLES BARKLEY**

"Charles loves golf so much he would play at half-time if he could, but I think a golf course is a waste of good pasture-land."

FELLOW NBA GREAT **KARL MALONE**

"One of the advantages bowling has over golf is that you seldom lose a bowling ball."

BOWLING LEGEND **DON CARTER**

"If you hit a bad shot, just tell yourself it is great to be alive, relaxing and walking around on a beautiful golf course. The next shot will be better."

AL GEIBERGER

"The most important shot in golf is the next one."

BEN HOGAN

"Concentrate, play your game, and don't be afraid to win."

AMY ALCOTT

"I'm an athlete. I may not look like it, but I'm an athlete. When I have to hook it around a tree, I just think, 'Hook it around a tree.' I don't get worried about it, I just do it. That's what my dad always said, 'Just play golf. If you hit a bad shot, hit the next one good.'"

BIG HITTER **BUBBA WATSON**

"Every shot counts. The three-foot putt is just as important as the 300-yard drive."

LEGENDARY BRITISH GOLFER **HENRY COTTON**

"Be decisive. A wrong decision is generally less disastrous than indecision."

BERNHARD LANGER

"Keep close count of your nickels and dimes, stay away from whiskey, and never concede a putt."

SAM SNEAD

"Keep your sense of humor. There's enough stress in the rest of your life not to let bad shots ruin a game you're supposed to enjoy."

AMY ALCOTT

"A bad attitude is worse than a bad swing."

PAYNE STEWART

"The number one thing about trouble is ... don't get into more."

DAVE STOCKTON

"If you can't outplay them, outwork them."

BEN HOGAN

"The golf gods do what they do."

COREY PAVIN, ATTEMPTING TO EXPLAIN HIS PGA TOUR NINE-HOLE RECORD 26 AT THE 2006 U.S. BANK CHAMPIONSHIP

"They say golf is like life, but don't believe them. Golf is more complicated than that."

LONGTIME PGA PRO AND SENIOR TOUR FOUNDER GARDNER DICKINSON

"Golf is deceptively simple, yet endlessly complicated."

ARNOLD PALMER

"I expect to make at least seven mistakes a round. Therefore, when I make a bad shot, I don't worry about it. It's just one of those seven."

WALTER HAGEN

"There's an old saying, 'It's a poor craftsman who blames his tools.' It's usually the player who misses those three-footers, not the putter."

KATHY WHITWORTH

"Golf giveth and golf taketh away, but it taketh away a hell of a lot more than it giveth."

SOUTH AFRICAN GOLFER SIMON HOBDAY

"Golf is like life in a lot of ways: The most important competition is the one against yourself. All the biggest wounds are self-inflicted. And you get a lot of breaks you don't deserve – both ways. So it's important not to get too upset when you're having a bad day."

PRESIDENT **BILL CLINTON**, ON WHAT HE LEARNED BY PLAYING GOLF

"Whoa, mama. Stay up!"

PRESIDENT **CLINTON** AFTER TEEING OFF DURING A VACATION IN 1993

"I know I am getting better at golf because I'm hitting fewer spectators."

PRESIDENT **GERALD FORD**

"I don't play for scores. I like to play fast."

PRESIDENT **GEORGE HERBERT WALKER BUSH**, WHOSE AIDES REFERRED TO HIS GAME AS "CART POLO"

"It does look like very good exercise,

but what is the little white ball for? "

UNITED STATES PRESIDENT **ULYSSES S. GRANT**

**"Whenever I play with Gerald Ford,
I try to make it a foursome –
the President,
myself,
a paramedic
and a faith healer."**

COMEDIAN **BOB HOPE**

"I would like to deny all allegations by Bob Hope that during my last game of golf, I hit an eagle, a birdie, an elk and a moose."

GERALD FORD

"President Eisenhower has given up golf for painting. It takes fewer strokes."

BOB HOPE

"Watching Sam Snead practice hitting golf balls is like watching a fish practice swimming."

JOHN SCHLEE

"They say Sam Snead is a natural golfer, but if he didn't practice he'd be a natural bad golfer."

GARY PLAYER

"No golfer can ever become too good to practice."

LEGENDARY BRITISH LADIES CHAMPION **MAY HEZLET**

"Don't be too proud to take lessons. I'm not."

JACK NICKLAUS

"The best exercise for golfers is golfing."

BOBBY JONES

"There is no such thing as a natural touch. Touch is something you create by hitting millions of golf balls."

LEE TREVINO

"Practice puts brains in your muscles."

SAM SNEAD

"There is nothing in this game of golf that can't be improved upon if you practice."

PATTY BERG

"It's a funny thing, the more I practice the luckier I get."

ARNOLD PALMER

"You must work very hard to become a natural golfer."

GARY PLAYER

"What a shame to waste those great shots on the practice tee."

WALTER HAGEN

"There are two things you can do with your head down – play golf and pray."

LEE TREVINO

"Prayer never works for me on the golf course. That may have something to do with my being a terrible putter."

REVEREND **BILLY GRAHAM**

"I never pray to God to make a putt. I pray to God to help me react good if I miss a putt."

CHI CHI RODRIGUEZ

"What a beautiful place a golf course is. From the meanest country pasture to the Pebble Beaches and St. Andrews of the world, a golf course is to me holy ground. I feel God in the trees and grass and flowers, in the rabbits and the birds and the squirrels, in the sky and the water. I feel that I am home."

LEGENDARY GOLF PRO AND INSTRUCTOR **HARVEY PENICK**

"Some of us worship in churches, some in synagogues, some on golf courses."

AMERICAN POLITICIAN **ADLAI STEVENSON**

"If you call on God to improve the results of a shot while it is still in motion, you are using 'an outside agency' and are subject to appropriate penalties under the rules of the game."

ENGLISH GOLF WRITER **HENRY LONGHUST**

"I wouldn't say God couldn't have gotten out of it, but he'd have had to throw it."

ARNOLD PALMER AFTER TROUBLE IN A BUNKER AT MUIRFIELD IN SCOTLAND

"I played golf with a priest the other day. He shot par-par-par-par-par. Finally I said to him, 'Father, if you're playing golf like this you haven't been saving many souls lately.'"

SAM SNEAD

"I'm gambling that when we get into the next life, Saint Peter will look at us and ask, 'Golfer?' And when we nod, he will step aside and say, 'Go right in; you've suffered enough.' One warning, if you do go in and the first thing you see is a par 3 surrounded by water, it ain't heaven."

LEGENDARY SPORTSWRITER **JIM MURRAY**

"There are two kinds of golf – golf and tournament golf. They are not the same."

BOBBY JONES

"There's a lot of pressure that comes with winning and I think I will deal with it a little better in the future.

I did this week. I handled myself great and played extremely well under the pressure."

BEN CURTIS, AFTER FINALLY COMPLETING A RAIN-DELAYED, WIRE-TO-WIRE VICTORY AT THE 2006 BOOZ ALLEN CLASSIC FOR HIS FIRST VICTORY SINCE WINNING THE 2003 BRITISH OPEN AS A ROOKIE

"Swinging at daisies is like playing electric guitar with a tennis racket: if it were that easy, we could all be Jerry Garcia. The ball changes everything."

GOLF WRITER **MICHAEL BAMBERGER**

"The game was easy for me as a kid. I had to play a while to find out how hard it is."

RAYMOND FLOYD

"Putts get real difficult the day they hand out the money."

LEE TREVINO

"It was so stressful out there. I felt like I needed an oxygen mask."

20-YEAR-OLD ROOKIE **JULIETA GRANADA** OF PARAGUAY, WHO WON THE 2006 SEASON-ENDING TOURNAMENT CHAMPIONSHIP AND EARNED $1 MILLION, THE BIGGEST PAYDAY IN LPGA HISTORY

"Over the years, I've studied the habits of golfers. I know what to look for. Watch their eyes. Fear shows up when there is an enlargement of the pupils. Big pupils lead to big scores."

SAM SNEAD

"Pressure is playing for $10 when you don't have a dime in your pocket."

LEE TREVINO

"I've heard people say putting is 50 percent technique and 50 percent mental. I really believe it is 50 percent technique and 90 percent positive thinking. See, but that adds up to 140 percent, which is why nobody is 100 percent sure how to putt."

CHI CHI RODRIGUEZ

"Putting is really a game within a game."

TOM WATSON

"Putting is like wisdom – partly a natural gift and partly an accumulation of experience."

ARNOLD PALMER

"Half of golf is fun. The other half is putting."

BRITISH GOLF COLUMNIST **PETER DOBEREINER**

"No putt is too short to be despised."

BOBBY JONES

"Putting greens are to golf courses what faces are to portraits."

AMATEUR GOLFER AND GOLF COURSE ARCHITECT
CHARLES BLAIR MacDONALD

"Retire to what? I'm a golfer and a fisherman. I've got no place to retire to."

JULIUS BOROS

"Baseball players quit playing and they take up golf. Basketball players quit, take up golf. Football players quit, take up golf. What are we supposed to take up when we quit?"

GEORGE ARCHER

"How has retirement affected my golf game? A lot more people beat me now."

FORMER PRESIDENT **DWIGHT D. EISENHOWER**

"I can say now that I'll know when I want to get out. But when I reach that time, I may not know."

JACK NICKLAUS SPEAKING OF RETIREMENT CIRCA 1979

"The people, they all want to see a good shot and you know it and you can't give them that good shot. That's when it's time."

ARNOLD PALMER, ANNOUNCING IN OCTOBER OF 2006
THAT HE WOULD NO LONGER PLAY COMPETITIVE GOLF
AFTER WITHDRAWING FROM A CHAMPION'S TOUR EVENT
EARLY IN THE FIRST ROUND

"Playing golf is a little like carving a turkey. It helps if you have your slice under control."

HUMORIST **BOB ORBEN**

"I don't say my golf game is bad, but if I grew tomatoes they'd come up sliced."

MILLER BARBER

"My swing is so bad I look like a caveman killing his lunch."

LEE TREVINO

"It's so bad I could putt off a tabletop and still leave the ball halfway down the leg."

J.C. SNEAD

"I hate a hook. It nauseates me. I could vomit. It's like a rattlesnake in your pocket."

BEN HOGAN

"You can talk to a fade but a hook won't listen."

LEE TREVINO

"Pretty similar. I lost all three."

ARNOLD PALMER, WHEN ASKED IF HIS PLAYOFF LOSS AT THE 1966 U.S. OPEN WAS SIMILAR TO THOSE IN 1962 AND 1963

"I expected to win again. It just took three years too long."

BEN CURTIS, AFTER WINNING THE RAIN-DELAYED 2006 BOOZ ALLEN CLASSIC FOR HIS FIRST VICTORY SINCE THE 2003 BRITISH OPEN

"Drink much beer. Big party."

JAPAN'S **YUSAKU MIYAZATO**, WHEN ASKED HOW HE PLANNED TO CELEBRATE AFTER TWO HOLE-IN-ONES DURING THE SAME ROUND AT THE 2006 PGA RENO-TAHOE OPEN

"If I had hit it like I wanted to I'd have holed it."

MARK CALCAVECCHIA

"Every week."

JEFF SLUMAN, KNOWN AS A SHORT HITTER, WHEN ASKED IF HE'S EVER PLAYED A COURSE HE THOUGHT WAS TOO LONG

"Because the other one didn't float."

CRAIG STADLER ON WHY HE SWITCHED PUTTERS

"Through years of experience I have found that air offers less resistance than dirt."

JACK NICKLAUS EXPLAINING WHEY HE TEES UP
A BALL SO HIGH

"How did I make a twelve on a par five hole? It's simple. I missed a four-foot-putt for an eleven."

ARNOLD PALMER

"I miss. I miss. I miss. I make."

SPANIARD **SEVE BALLESTEROS**, DESCRIBING HIS
FOUR-PUTT ON NO. 16 AT AUGUSTA IN 1988

"My handicap? Woods and irons."

BASEBALL PLAYER **CHRIS CODIROLI**

"Golf swings are like snowflakes: there are no two exactly alike."

PETER JACOBSEN

"The golf swing is like a suitcase into which we are trying to pack one too many things. "

WRITER **JOHN UPDIKE**

"Reverse every natural instinct and do the opposite of what you are inclined to do, and you will probably come very close to having a perfect golf swing."

BEN HOGAN

"Dividing the swing into its parts is like dissecting a cat. You'll have blood and guts and bones all over the place. But you won't have a cat."

BRITISH GOLFER **ERNEST JONES** WHO BECAME ONE OF THE GAME'S FIRST GREAT INSTRUCTORS

"The point is that it doesn't matter if you look like a beast before or after the hit, as long as you look like a beauty at the moment of impact."

SEVE BALLESTEROS

"**Don't be in such a hurry. That little white ball isn't going to run away from you.**"

PATTY BERG

"The only thing you should force in a golf swing is the club back into the bag."

BYRON NELSON

"I used to get out there and have a thousand swing thoughts. Now I try not to have any."

DAVIS LOVE III

"You don't hit anything on the backswing, so why rush it?"

DOUG FORD

"I still swing the way I used to, but when I look up the ball is going in a different direction."

LEE TREVINO

"You can buy a country but you can't buy a golf swing. It's not on the shelf."

GENE SARAZEN

"The golf swing is among the most stressful and unnatural acts in sports, short of cheering for the Yankees."

PGA TOUR PRO AND RED SOX FAN **BRAD FAXON**

"One minute it's fear and loathing, but hit a couple of good shots and you're on top of the world. I've gone crazy over this game."

ACTOR **JACK NICHOLSON**

"Golf is a search for perfection, for balance. It's about meditation and concentration."

SINGER **CÉLINE DION**

"With the sax, I learned technique well enough so that it feels like part of my body and I just express myself. That's where I want to get in golf."

SAXOPHONIST **KENNY G**, WHO WAS RANKED AS THE #1 GOLFER IN *GOLF DIGEST*'S TOP 100 IN MUSIC IN 2006

"I get way more nervous playing golf in front of 500 people than being on stage in front of 20,000 people."

SINGER **JUSTIN TIMBERLAKE**

"I'm the worst golfer in the world and the worst singer in the world and I love both of those. Maybe I should sing while I'm playing golf."

ACTOR **JAMIE FARR**

"One day I did get angry with myself and threw a club. My caddy told me, 'You're not good enough to get mad.'"

ACTOR **SAMUEL L. JACKSON**

"I always thought of myself as some sort of athlete until I started playing golf a couple years ago."

ACTOR **JAMES CAAN**

"Musicians and golfers understand each other. We know what it takes to have to perform. We know there is a lot of alone time."

COUNTRY MUSIC STAR, AND SCRATCH GOLFER, **VINCE GILL**

"Golf takes me out of the crap of a sick world. Golfers are genuinely courteous in a discourteous world. Show me a guest on *The Jerry Springer Show* who's a golfer."

ACTOR **JAMES WOODS**

"It was cool for a couple of weeks, but how much bad golf can you play?"

ACTOR **JOHN GOODMAN**

"The real reason your pro tells you to keep your head down

is so you can't see him laughing at you."

COMEDIAN PHYLLIS DILLER

"There isn't a flaw in his golf or his makeup. He will win more majors than Arnold Palmer and me combined. Somebody is going to dust my records. It might as well be Tiger, because he's such a great kid."

JACK NICKLAUS

"You know, he's got an uncanny ability, when somebody gets close to him, to just turn it up another level."

CHRIS DIMARCO ON TIGER WOODS, WHO BEAT HIM BY TWO STROKES AT THE 2006 BRITISH OPEN

"It's been a fun challenge for me and the other guys, and he's also pushed me to work harder and get better and achieve levels of success I may not have achieved had he not been there pushing me."

PHIL MICKELSON, PUTTING A POSITIVE SPIN ON HIS SOMETIMES HEATED RIVALRY WITH TIGER WOODS

"I've always played all right when I've played with him. I think it's very easy to get caught up watching him play because it's so much fun. All of a sudden you're on the sixth hole and haven't really paid attention to what you're doing."

2006 U.S. OPEN CHAMPION **GEOFF OGILVY** ON PLAYING WITH TIGER WOODS

"I made a couple of putts. The rest of the time I could've just watched."

JIM FURYK, ON THE FIRST TIME HE WAS PAIRED WITH TIGER WOODS

"I tell you what, if I had his game, you could analyze it eight days a week, 25 hours a day. I wouldn't care. Are you kidding me?"

RICH BEEM, ON THE CONSTANT SCRUTINY TIGER WOODS FACES

"I get to play golf for a living. What more can you ask than getting paid for doing what you love?"

TIGER WOODS

"I've learned to trust the subconscious. My instincts have never lied to me."

TIGER WOODS

"I don't intend to do it on purpose. That's not one of those things where I can turn on the switch. I believe in the way I play golf, that you turn on the switch on the first hole and you have it on the entire time."

TIGER WOODS, DENYING THAT HE CAN TURN UP HIS GAME WHEN THE COMPETITION GETS CLOSE

"I always feel pressure. If you don't feel nervous, that means you don't care about how you play. I care about how I perform. I've always said the day I'm not nervous playing is the day I quit."

TIGER WOODS

"I did envisage being this successful as a player, but not all the hysteria around it off the golf course."

TIGER WOODS

"I feel in control of my golf ball."

TIGER WOODS, WHILE EN ROUTE TO HIS FIFTH STRAIGHT TOURNAMENT WIN IN 2006

"He thoroughly enjoyed watching me grind out major championships. I know this one would have brought a smile to his face."

TIGERS WOODS, AFTER BATTLING TO WIN THE 2006 BRITISH OPEN IN HIS FIRST MAJOR AFTER THE DEATH OF HIS FATHER EARL

"Unfortunately, the suit is so stiff, I can't do this with two hands, but I'm going to try a little sand-trap shot here."

ALAN SHEPARD, GOLF ENTHUSIAST AND COMMANDER OF APOLLO 14, DESCRIBING HIS FIRST ATTEMPT TO DRIVE A GOLF BALL ON THE MOON

"Got more dirt than ball. Here we go again."

ALAN SHEPARD, PREPARING TO TAKE ANOTHER SWING

"The suit was so clumsy, being pressurized, it was impossible to get two hands comfortably on the handle and it's impossible to make any kind of a turn. It was kind of a one-handed chili-dip."

ALAN SHEPARD DESCRIBING THE DIFFICULTY OF HIS MOON SHOT TO *OTTAWA GOLF* MAGAZINE

"Then I thought, with the same clubhead speed, the ball's going to go at least six times as far. There's absolutely no drag, so if you do happen to spin it, it won't slice or hook 'cause there's no atmosphere to make it turn."

ALAN SHEPARD DESCRIBING THE ADVANTAGES OF HIS MOON SHOT TO *OTTAWA GOLF* MAGAZINE

"Miles and miles and miles."

ALAN SHEPARD DESCRIBING THE FLIGHT OF
HIS SECOND GOLF SHOT ON THE MOON

"A couple of weeks ago I went fishing and on the first cast I missed the lake."

BEN CRENSHAW DURING A SLUMP

"I putted like Joe Schmoe, and I'm not even sure Joe would appreciate that."

ARNOLD PALMER AFTER A BAD ROUND

"I'm hitting the ball so terrible, I'm too disgusted to even practice."

MARK CALCAVECCHIA

"My game is so bad I gotta hire three caddies: one to walk the left rough, one for the right rough, and one down the middle. And the one in the middle doesn't have much to do."

DAVE HILL

"My luck is so bad that if I bought a cemetery people would stop dying."

ED FURGOL

"When someone has a bad day like that on the golf course, you say, Greg, you look good, you look fantastic.

I like your shoes, I like your pants,

I like your ... well,

the hat's okay.

I mean, you need to keep it light. Instead they say, Greg, what's next?

Suicide? Alcoholism? Drugs?"

ACTOR **BILL MURRAY** ON THE MEDIA'S BLUDGEONING OF GREG NORMAN AFTER HIS 1996 MASTERS COLLAPSE

"If I'm on the course and lightning starts,

I get inside fast.

If God wants to play through, let him. "

COMEDIAN BOB HOPE

"When the ducks are walking, you know it is too windy to be playing golf."

DAVE STOCKTON

"When it's breezy, hit it easy."

DAVIS LOVE, JR.

"Well, I'm glad we don't have to play in the shade."

BOBBY JONES AFTER BEING TOLD IT WAS MORE THAN 100 DEGREES IN THE SHADE

"The wind was so strong, there were whitecaps in the porta-john."

JOYCE KAZMIERSKI AFTER A STORMY ROUND AT THE 1983 WOMEN'S KEMPER OPEN

"The only things I fear on a golf course are lightning and Ben Hogan."

SAM SNEAD

"What does it take to be a champion? Desire, dedication determination, concentration and the will to win."

PATTY BERG

"It's not whether you win or lose, but whether I win or lose."

SANDY LYLE

"Show me a man who is a good loser and I'll show you a man who is playing golf with his boss."

LEGENDARY SPORTSWRITER **JIM MURRAY**

"Great champions learn from past experiences, whether those be good or bad. A lot of times a guy needs to be knocked down before he gets up and fights."

PAUL AZINGER

"You hear that winning breeds winning. But no, winners are bred from losing. They learn they don't like it."

TOM WATSON

"A competitor will find a way to win. Competitors take bad breaks and use them to drive themselves just that much harder. Quitters take bad breaks and use them as reasons to give up. It's all a matter of pride."

NANCY LOPEZ

"I still get the butterflies on the first tee. I still get sweaty hands, and my heart pumps a lot going down the 18th. But I know what winning is all about now, and that's a feeling that I like."

ANNIKA SORENSTAM

"To be a champion, you have to find a way to get the ball in the cup on the last day."

TOM WATSON

"My main goal starting the day was to go out there and win the golf tournament."

VIJAY SINGH

"Tournaments are won on Sunday and on the back nine."

JACK NICKLAUS

"You cannot be thinking of winning a tournament. It's only Thursday. I'm just trying to put myself in a good position for Sunday."

LORENA OCHOA, IN CONTENTION TO WIN THE 2006 LPGA TOURNAMENT OF CHAMPIONS, AND BATTLING KARRIE WEBB AND ANNIKA SORENSTAM FOR PLAYER OF THE YEAR HONORS (SHE WON BOTH TOURNAMENT AND PLAYER OF THE YEAR)

"To play well on the final holes of a major championship, you need a certain arrogance. You have to
   find a trance, some kind of self-hypnosis that's
   almost a state of grace."

   HALE IRWIN

"A great round of golf is like a terrible round. You
   drift into a zone, and it's hard to break out of it."

   AL GEIBERGER

"When I play my best golf, I feel as if I'm in a fog,
   standing back watching the earth in orbit with a
   golf club in my hands."

   LPGA LEGEND **MICKEY WRIGHT**

"The zone is the ability to give 110 percent of your
   attention and your focus to the shot. When I'm on
   the tee, I'll see a divot in the fairway and try to run
   my ball over that divot – and succeed. That's the
   zone."

   NICK PRICE

"**As far as swing and techniques are concerned, I don't know diddly squat. When I'm playing well, I don't even take aim.**"

FRED COUPLES

cover: Stan Honda/AFP/Getty Images; title page: Getty Images; 8 Mike Powell/Allsport/Getty Images; 12 Timothy A. Clary/AFP/Getty Images; 16 Martha Holmes/Time Life Pictures/Getty Images; 19 Lynn Pelham/ Time Life Pictures/Getty Images; 22 Mike Powell/Getty Images; 26 Scott Halleran/Getty Images; 30 Don Morley/Getty Images; 33 Richard Heathcote/Getty Images; 34 David Cannon/Getty Images; 39 Jeff Haynes/AFP/Getty Images; 42 Scott Halleran/Getty Images; 45 Focus on Sport/Getty Images; 48 Jeff Vinnick/Getty Images; 54 Jonathan Ferrey/Getty Images; 57 Joseph Scherschel/Time Life Pictures/Getty Images; 58 Warren Little/Getty Images; 61 Ross Kinnaird/Getty Images; 62 Andrew Redington/Getty Images; 66 Adrian Dennis/AFP/Getty Images; 69 Brian Morgan/Getty Images; 72 Andy Lyons/Getty Images; 77 Warren Little/Getty Images; 78 Andrew Redington/Getty Images; 81 Simon Bruty/Allsport; 86 Dominic Favre/AFP/Getty Images; 92 Jamie Squire/Getty Images; 99 Ken Levine/Allsport; 101 Jeff Gross/Getty Images; 109 Kirby/Topical Press Agency/Getty Images; 111 Adrian Dennis/AFP/Getty Images; 114 Jeff Gross/Getty Images; 118 Adrian Dennis/AFP/Getty Images; 121 Tony Feder/Getty Images; 123 Time Life Pictures/White House/Time Life Pictures/Getty Images; 128 New York Times Co./Getty Images; 133 Scott Halleran/Getty Images; 134 David Cannon/Allsport/Getty Images; 138 Scott Halleran/Getty Images; 142 Harry How/Getty Images; 146 Becker/Fox Photos/Getty Images; 149 Justin Sullivan/Getty Images; 153 Richard Heathcote/Getty Images; 157 Andy Lyons/Allsport/Getty Images; 159 Ralph Morse/Time Life Pictures/Getty Images; 164 Alan Grant/Time Life Pictures/Getty Images; 169 Jeff Haynes/AFP/Getty Images

Eric Zweig is an author, editor and sports historian. He has written articles for the *Toronto Star*, the *Globe and Mail* and the *Toronto Sun* and appeared on CBC Television's "Hockey: A People's History." He is also the author or editor of dozens of sports books, including *Home Plate Don't Move: Baseball's Best Quotes and Quips* and *Gentlemen, This is a Football: Football's Best Quotes and Quips*. Unfortunately, his work schedule (and a serious lack of skill!) leaves him with few opportunities to hit the links.